SILENT COMPASSION

Silent Compassion

Finding God in Contemplation

RICHARD ROHR

franciscan
media®
Cincinnati, Ohio

Scripture quotes are from the author's own translation.

Cover and book design by Mark Sullivan.

ISBN 978-1-63253-413-2

Published by Franciscan Media
28 W. Liberty St.
Cincinnati, OH 45202
www.FranciscanMedia.org

Printed in the United States of America.
23 24 25 26 27   5 4 3 2 1

CONTENTS

FOREWORD

"If we stay silent for a whole hour," Richard Rohr asserts in this dynamic meditation on contemplative life, "it will be hard not to write a poem."

Oh, how I love this statement. He could have written, "It is in silence that we come into the presence of God," or "Silence yields to the spaces between the words." And he has said things like this. So has almost every contemplative teacher on the planet. But there is something utterly fresh and penetrating in Father Rohr's affirmation that deep quiet invites us to perceive the world as saturated in meaning and brimming with metaphor. We see the face of the Holy shining from this Jack Russel Terrier and this bruised banana, within the first snow of the season and inside the trail of moonlight on water, in the electric embrace of a lover and in the heartbreak of a lover leaving. In silence, we learn to recognize the universal nestled in the particular, yes, and we also come to appreciate the riot of diversity that flows from the fountain of that singular source. As a poet myself, I know exactly what Rohr means when he challenges us to try not writing a poem in response to any deep encounter with silence!

Silent Compassion is an ingathering of Rohr's reflections on the luminous thread of love that unites all spiritual traditions at their heart, a connective filament we are unlikely to recognize until we become still enough to allow it to reveal itself. This book is the ripened fruit of a seed that sprouted when two great religious leaders, Father Richard Rohr and His Holiness the Dalai Lama, taught together in 2013 at the Festival of Faiths in Louisville, Kentucky, just down the road from Gethsemani Abbey where, a half century earlier, Thomas Merton experienced the perennial philosophy flowering from the garden of his own contemplative life.

In their own ways, both His Holiness and Father Rohr exemplify the sincere desire to lean so closely toward the other that all otherness disappears. It is this orientation of the heart that gave rise to the distilled wisdom offered here. "The divisions, dichotomies, and dualisms of the world can only be overcome by a unitive consciousness at every level: personal, relational, social, political, cultural, in interreligious dialogue, and particularly in spirituality," Rohr writes in his Introduction. "This is the unique and central job of healthy religion." Richard Rohr has spent a lifetime in the joyous pursuit and generous sharing of the glorious "and" that links contemplation with action, personal with collective, Christianity with every other great wisdom tradition across the ages and around the world. It conjoins the words Silent with Compassion in the title of this book.

At the heart of this offering is an invitation to be still. Such stillness, however, is not a barren field, devoid of substance. It is a silence replete with beauty. It is what Buddhism refers to as sunyata, the boundlessness that characterizes the truth of existence. We do not taste this truth by transcending our embodied experience and dropping into some kind of detached trance where nothing worldly can touch us. Rather, it is a dynamic state of nondual consciousness in which we experience our felt connection with all of life, rather than spouting compelling arguments for ontological unity. Rohr's teachings on the power of silence uncover the network of "interbeing," as Vietnamese Zen Buddhist teacher Thich Nhat Hanh (1926–2022) described it, and invite us to take our rightful place in the middle of it all. From this vantage point, it is impossible not to see the earth herself as a beloved relative and to claim our kinship with all creation—human and animal, wind and fire, even death—as Rohr's own spiritual father Francis of Assisi did. "God [is] a dynamic flow," Rohr teaches, "a communion, relationship itself."

There seems to be something universally enthralling about silence and stillness. We both fear it and yearn for it. I believe— and I think Rohr would agree—that whoever dares to sit down and get quiet qualifies as a contemplative. Across the spiritual traditions and outside of any particular religious affiliation, we crave "the peace that surpasses all understanding" (Philippians 4:7), and whenever we are lucky enough to encounter it, we take refuge there. This is not a peace that delivers us from mundane existence but instead bubbles up from the wellspring of everyday life. Rather than using prayer and meditation to rescue us from the human condition, we engage contemplative practices to metabolize and integrate our experiences and become more intimate with the Divine Presence that is always available to us. As Rohr has often noted, "many come to the contemplative mind as the fruit of great suffering or great love." In other words, when we embrace Reality, Reality takes us into its arms and reveals its essential divinity.

This is not some fluffy, postmodern platitude to hawk in the spiritual marketplace. It is the quintessence of what Rohr calls the alternative orthodoxy. It is a truth that resounds from the heart of all the world's great mystical traditions. It is a lived and living wisdom that welcomes everything and everybody and leaves nothing and nobody out. That means you. As Rohr notes, "Organized religion usually tells us that mystical union with God is possible, but we should not really expect it. We're told that's only for special people. This ends up making mystical moments something very elitist, distant, and only available to a few now and then."

We must release spirituality from the prison of religiosity. This involves "looking out from a different set of eyes, which are not comparing, competing, judging, labeling, or analyzing, but receiving the moment in its present wholeness and incompleteness." Contemplative life is a matter of cultivating this loving gaze.

It is one of the great joys and honors of my lifetime to be able to call Richard Rohr my friend. I would be hard pressed to name another teacher who has had a greater influence on the consciousness of an entire generation, both within his home tradition of Christianity and far beyond. He embodies that rare and beautiful blend of radical humility and quiet authority, rooted in his own lived experience of great love and great suffering. In the pages of this book, you can find the distilled elixir of his most profound and grounded insights. Although each chapter spills graciously into the one before and culminates in a brimming basin of practical wisdom, I encourage you to approach this book as you would an oracle, opening it anywhere and drinking in the living waters of that page as the precise remedy you need for any given moment of your life. Silent Compassion unveils the Perennial Tradition in full color. It is contemplative wisdom in action.

Mirabai Starr

Taos, New Mexico

January 2023

The Perennial Tradition

In mid-May 2013, I was honored to teach in Louisville, Kentucky, alongside His Holiness the Dalai Lama and other religious leaders at the Festival of Faiths, a program of public events intended to nurture interfaith dialogue and build a respectful, unified community.

Fifty years after Thomas Merton (1915–1968) traveled to Southeast Asia from the nearby Abbey of Gethsemani and walked and talked with the young Dalai Lama (days before Merton's tragic accidental death), the Dalai Lama had traveled to Kentucky to share a stage with Christians, Muslims, Hindus, Jews, and other Buddhists.

The Dalai Lama came to Louisville on a type of world tour, not only to build support for the oppressed people of Tibet, but also to spread his own message of peace and mysticism, a blend of action and contemplation built on an ancient and perennial tradition that has characterized his life.

Joining him on that stage, I thought of my spiritual father, Francis of Assisi (1181–1226), who traveled perilous thirteenth-century roads to meet with the sultan of Egypt, Saladin's nephew, to preach peace and interfaith understanding. While Francis' peace mission was unsuccessful, he and the sultan found common ground in that perennial tradition, just as Thomas Merton and I did with the Dalai Lama.

The perennial philosophy, or perennial tradition, is a concept that has come in and out of popularity in Western and religious history, but it has never been dismissed by the Christian Church. In many ways, it was actually affirmed at the Second Vatican Council in its forward-looking documents on ecumenism (*Unitatis Redintegratio*) and non-Christian religions (*Nostra Aetate*). It affirms that there are some constant themes, truths, and recurrences in all the world religions.

In *Nostra Aetate*, for example, the Council Fathers began by stating that "One is the community of all peoples, one their origin, for God made the whole human race to live over the face of the earth. One also is their final goal, God.... The Catholic Church rejects nothing which is true and holy in these religions."[1] The document goes on to state that Native religion, Hinduism, Judaism, Buddhism, and Islam "reflect a ray of that Truth which enlightens all."[2] We need to realize what courage and brilliance it took to write that in 1965, when very few people in any religion thought that way. In fact, most still don't think that way today.

One early exception was the great St. Augustine (354–430), a Doctor of the Church, who courageously wrote: "For what is now called the Christian religion existed even among the ancients and was not lacking from the beginning of the human race until 'Christ came in the flesh.' From that time, true religion, which already existed, began to be called Christian."[3] St. Clement of Alexandria, Origen, St. Basil, St. Gregory of Nyssa, and St. Leo the Great all held similar understandings before we got into the defensive (and offensive!) modes of anti-Semitism and the Crusades. In some crucial ways, we have actually gone backward in religious history when we should have been greasing the wheels of spiritual consciousness to move forward.

The perennial tradition is approximately referenced in the council's decree on priestly formation (*Optatam Totius*), which states that seminarians should be "relying on a philosophy... which is perennially valid," and the decree encourages study of the entire history of philosophy and also "recent progress of the sciences."[4] The authors were probably thinking primarily of Scholastic philosophy. In truth, our term, as I use it here, is much more a theological statement than a philosophical one, anyway. This was the understanding of Aldous Huxley (1894–1963), which is why he called it a metaphysic, a psychology, and an ethic at the same time:

> The metaphysic that recognizes a divine Reality substantial
> to the world of things and lives and minds; the psychology

that finds in the soul something similar to, or even iden-
tical with, divine Reality; the ethic that places man's final
end in the knowledge of the immanent and transcendent Ground of all being—the thing is immemorial and
universal. Rudiments of the Perennial Philosophy may be
found among the traditionary lore of primitive peoples in
every region of the world, and in its fully developed forms
it has a place in every one of the higher religions.[5]

The divisions, dichotomies, and dualisms of the world can only
be overcome by a unitive consciousness at every level: personal,
relational, social, political, cultural, in interreligious dialogue,
and particularly in spirituality. This is the unique and central job
of healthy religion (*re-ligio* means "re-ligament").

As Jesus put it in his great final prayer, "I pray that all may be
one" (John 17:21). Or, as my favorite Christian mystic, Lady
Julian of Norwich (1342–1416) wrote, "By myself I am nothing
at all, but in general, I am in the *oneing* of love. For it is in this
oneing that the life of all people exists."[6]

Many teachers have made the central, but frequently missed,
point that unity is not the same as uniformity. Unity, in fact,
is the reconciliation of differences, and those differences must
be maintained—and yet overcome! We must actually distinguish
and separate things before we can spiritually unite them, usually
at some cost to ourselves (see Ephesians 2:14–16). If only we had

made that simple clarification, so many problems—and over-emphasized, separate identities—could have moved to a much higher level of love and service.

Paul already made this universal principle very clear in several of his letters. For example, "There is a variety of gifts, but it is always the same Spirit. There are all sorts of service to be done, but always to the same Lord, working in all sorts of different ways in different people. It is the same God working in all of them" (1 Corinthians 12:4–6). In his community at Ephesus, they were taught, "There is one Lord, one faith, one baptism, one God who is Father of all, over all, through all, and within all, and each one of us has been given our own share of grace" (Ephesians 4:5–7).

We must finally go back to the ultimate Christian source for our principle: the central doctrine of the Trinity itself. Yes, God is one, just as our Jewish ancestors taught us (see Deuteronomy 6:4), and yet the further, subtler level is that this oneness is, in fact, the radical love union between the three completely distinct persons of the Trinity. The basic principle and problem of the one and the many is overcome in God's very nature. God is a mystery of relationship, and the truest relationship is love. The three are not uniform but quite distinct, yet completely unified in total outpouring.

Further, our word *person*, now referring to an individual human being, was actually first used in Greek-based Trinitarian theology (*persona* means "stage mask" or a "sounding through"), and later then applied also to us. So, we are not autonomous beings, but soundings through. We are apart, but radically one too, just as Father, Son, and Holy Spirit are. The implications could make for years of meditation. We really are created in God's "image and likeness" (Genesis 1:26–27), much more than we ever imagined. Trinity is our universal template for the nature of reality and for how to become *one*.

As dear Julian wrote, "The love of God creates in us such a *oneing* that when it is truly seen, no person can separate themselves from another person,"[7] and "In the sight of God, all humans are *oned*, and one person is all people, and all people are in one person."[8]

This is not some twenty-first-century flabby fabrication. This is not pantheism or New Age optimism. This is the whole point: it was, indeed, supposed to usher in a new age—and still will and can. This is the perennial tradition. Our job is not to discover it, but to retrieve what has been discovered—and enjoyed—again and again, in the mystics and saints of all religions.

As John the Beloved wrote, "I do not write to you because you do not know the truth, but because you know it already" (1 John 2:21).

CHAPTER ONE

Finding God in the Depths of Silence

People who are interested in peace and justice surely recognize how communication, vocabulary, and conversation have deteriorated in our society. We are aware of this in our politics, and we are aware of it in our churches too. It feels as though the only way through this is a re-appreciation for this wonderful, but seemingly harmless, thing called silence.

How do we market that which is inherently unmarketable? How do we "sell" silence? How do we make attractive what feels like selling air or selling emptiness or selling something that, certainly to the capitalistic mind, would not immediately be attractive at all? I believe we must try anyway.

Silence is not just what happens around words and underneath images and events. It has a life of its own. It's a phenomenon with an almost physical identity. It is a being in itself, to which we can relate. Philosophically, we would say *being* is that foundational quality which precedes all other attributes. When we relate to the naked being of a thing, we learn to know it at its core. Silence is somehow at the very foundation of all reality. It is that out of which all being comes and to which all things return. (If the word *silence* does not grab you, you can interchange it with nothingness, emptiness, vastness, formlessness, open space, and so on.)

What we do know is that all things are *creatio ex nihilo*—that every something, by God's plan, first comes from nothing. If we can first rest in the nothing, we will then be prepared to appreciate the something. When nothing creates something, we call it grace.

Such silence was described in the very first two verses of the Book of Genesis. The first reality is described as a "formless void," and the Spirit is "hovering" over this silent void. The Spirit is silent, but powerful, and the coming together of these two great silences is the beginning of our creation, at least in the Judeo-Christian story.

Silence precedes, undergirds, and grounds everything. We cannot just see it as an accident, or as something unnecessary. But unless we learn how to live there, go there, abide in this different phenomenon, the rest of things—words, events, relationships, identities—all become rather superficial, without depth or context. They lose meaning. All we search for is a life of more events, more situations which must increasingly contain ever-higher stimulation, more excitement, and more color, to add vital signs to our inherently bored and boring existence. The simplest and most stripped-down things really do have the power to give us the greatest happiness—if we respect them as such. Silence is the essence of simple and stripped down.

This need for stimulation is part of the character of America and most Western countries. We must be honest about this. There are so many signs of cultural deterioration all around us. Everything has to be a little louder, a little brighter, a little newer, a little more expensive, a little classier, and especially a little quicker. Then the Americans will come. It is not "If you build it, they will come," but "If you make it fancy, they will come." We have grown used to this. We accept as normative what even the Roman emperors knew to be a sign of decline: "Bread and circuses are all this people need or want," they said. Here in America, we close schools and build sports stadiums that look like cathedrals.

One of the most important experiences for me has been to teach in so many developing countries, where I came to the realization that most of the world does not live the way we live—but, sadly, they want to!

We must not think of American culture as the norm or the goal. This is not necessarily a healthy society. We are not necessarily the best culture or the greatest, although I know Americans are trained to think that way. It is easy to think that way only if we have never been outside of America. We surely have some wonderful aspects to our society and some very unhealthy aspects too, one of which is that we do not consider silence as attractive, useful, necessary, important, or even good. Over time, we have become more of a shell, with less and less inside or in the depths of things—where all the vitality is to be found.

We need to experience silence as a living presence in itself, which is primordial and primal, and then see all other things—now experienced deeply—inside of that container. Silence is not just an absence, but also, by that very fact, a presence. Silence surrounds every "I know" event with a humble and patient "I don't know." It protects the autonomy and dignity of events, persons, animals, and all things.

We must find a way to return to this place, to live in this place, to abide in this place of inner silence. Outer silence means very little if there is not a deeper inner silence. Everything else appears much clearer when it appears or emerges out of a previous silence. When I use the word *appear*, I mean that silence takes on reality, substance, significance, or meaning. Without silence around a thing, which is a mystery, nothing has meaning—or a meaning that lasts. It is just another event in a sequence of ever-quicker events, which we call our lives.

Without silence, we do not really experience our experiences. We have many experiences, but they do not have the power to change us, to awaken us, or, as Jesus says, to give us that peace that the world cannot give (see John 14:27).

To live in this primordial, foundational being itself, which I am calling silence, creates a kind of sympathetic resonance with what is right in front of us. Without it, we are reacting instead of responding. Without some degree of silence, we are never living, never tasting, as there is not much capacity to enjoy, or to appreciate, or to experience the moment. The opposite of contemplation is not action, it is reaction. We must wait for pure action, which always proceeds from a contemplative silence.

Silence is not the absence of being, but it is a kind of being itself. It is not something distant or obscure, of which only ascetics are capable. Rather, you may have already experienced deep silence, and now you must feed it, free it, and allow it to become light within you. We do not hear silence (precisely!), but it is that by which we do hear. We cannot capture silence. It captures us.

Silence is a kind of thinking that is not thinking. It is a kind of thinking which sees (*contemplata* means "to see"). Silence, then, is an alternative consciousness. It is a form of intelligence, a form of knowing beyond bodily reacting, which is what we normally call *emotion*. It is a form of knowing beyond mental analysis, which is what we usually call *thinking*.

By the age of seven, almost all of us have separated our body and our soul from our mind, and we give all our credence to our mind, disconnected from our bodies and souls, which abide and grow in silence.

René Descartes (1596–1650) was not wrong when he stated, "I think, therefore I am." He was accurately describing the Western person. Our thinking is who we *think* we are, but we are so much more than our thoughts about things.

All the great world religions at the higher levels have discovered that this tyrannical mode of thinking has to be relativized, has to be limited, or it completely takes over—to the loss of our primal being. Pretty soon, words mean less and less. They mean whatever we want them to mean (we must be honest here). But this leads to more and more cynicism and suspicion about all words, even our own. In our postmodern culture, we all use words to mean what we want—so that we can get what we want. It is an incestuous circle.

Listen to the character of whatever political debate emerges in America: guns, health care, war, or the most recent reality show. The words on either side mean less and less in terms of objective truth. We have all come to recognize this. It becomes a game that we all are forced to play. The only way out is often to be silent—like Jesus before Pilate (see Mark 15:5; John 19:9).

The soul does not use words. It surrounds words with space, and that is what I mean by silence.

The ego, on the other hand, uses words to get what it wants. When we are in an argument with our spouses, friends, or colleagues, that is what we do. We pull out the words that give us power. We pull out the words that make us look right, superior, and intelligent and that we think will help us win the argument. We all have done it. It is all the ego knows how to do. But words at that level are rather useless and even dishonest and destructive.

The filling of space with words and sound is now called entertainment. Even there, we too often focus on events that are tragic, or that will draw forth sentiment or reaction. We call that *urgent* news, which we know is often manufactured by the emotion of the newscaster's voice. At that point, we are three steps removed from contact with reality.

This is what inevitably happens when there is no appreciation for silence, when the silence around the words is not just as important, or maybe even more important, than the choosing of the words themselves.

Silence is a kind of wholeness. It can absorb contraries. It can absorb paradoxes and contradictions. Maybe that is why we do not like silence. There is nothing to argue about in true inner silence, and the mind likes to argue. It gives us something to do.

Often, our interactions lead to argumentation, even within the church, and even about the forms of prayer. Take the issues of inclusive language and male or female leadership, which are indeed important questions. Do I like that psalm, or is this psalm too violent? Is that singing too Evangelical or too Catholic or too charismatic? There has to be an issue with something, or I hardly feel useful. That is one reason why contemplative prayer, especially in a group, is so liberating and calming. There are no sides to take.

It comes down to this: the ego loves a situation where it can take sides, and true interior silence really does not allow us to take sides. I describe this common tendency as *dualistic thinking* and not contemplation itself.

We can see how someone who lives in a capitalist culture in which everything is about competing, comparing, and winning, will find silence counterintuitive. How do we teach something as empty, as harmless, and as certain to create failure as silence? We will do it only when we know that it also offers a "peace beyond understanding" (Philippians 4:7) and a "joy that no one can take from you" (John 16:22).

If those in the church limit their focus to the external techniques and formulas with which most liturgy becomes preoccupied (e.g., how the priests' hands are folded, what words they are saying, and what types of vestments they are wearing), the soul remains largely untouched and unchanged. Too much emphasis on what I will call "social prayer" or wordy prayer gives us far too much to argue about, and that is surely why Jesus emphasized the quiet prayer in our own "inner room" and told us not to "babble on as the pagans do" (Matthew 6:5–7).

What I have experienced during my longer Lenten retreats is that time seems to increase inside of silence. It feels like time "coming to fullness," in Christian Scripture terms: time beyond time. It shifts from the Greek *chronos*, from each successive moment of chronological time, to *kairos*, or momentous time, when one moment is as perfect as it can be. Then it is all right here, right now. It is enough. I am more than okay. I am content.

If we can experience silence as the ground and birth of all words, then we will find that when we speak, our words will be well chosen and calm.

Francis told us to always use words that were "well chosen and chaste." In other words, we should not preach unless we have something to say. We are not to preach just to be preaching. For Francis, all preaching was to be the direct fruit of contemplation, not just idle ideas.

When we recognize something as beautiful, it partly emerges from the silence around it. It may be why we are quiet in art galleries. If something is not surrounded by the vastness of silence and space, it is hard to appreciate it. If something is all mixed in with everything else, then its singularity, as a unique and beautiful object, does not stand out.

Silence needs to be understood in a larger way than simply a lack of audible sound or a lack of noise. Whenever emptiness— what seems like empty space, the absence of sound—becomes its own kind of fullness with its own kind of sweet voice, we have experienced what I mean by silence.

I read years ago that silence is the net below the tightrope walker. As we walk, we try to find the right words to explain our experience, but silence is the safety net that allows us to fall. It admits, as poets often do, that no word will ever be perfectly right or sufficient. So, like the poet, we keep trying. The great spaciousness and safety net beneath the tightrope walker frees them from self-preoccupation and fear of making a mistake. Like the net beneath the tightrope, the silence upholds us, surrounds our mistakes, and gives us more space to correct them.

There are two kinds of silence. There is the natural, refreshing silence of the introverted personality or the pause between conversations. But there is also a spiritual silence that does not need to be filled with nervous laughter or a joke, or any attempt to be clever or show that we are informed and an insider. Such spiritual silence demands a deep presence to ourselves and others in the moment.

If life is primarily words and ideas—and that is what we have made it into, especially after the invention of the printing press, then death—that great mystery that we haven't walked through yet—is silence. Therefore, we could say that faith and silence are both a practicing for death. Who am I before—and after—all of my words, ideas, and understandings?

I began my book *Immortal Diamond* with these epigraphs:

The fact that life and death are "not two" is extremely difficult to grasp, not because it is so complex, but because it is so simple.
—Ken Wilber

We miss the unity of life and death at the very point where our ordinary mind begins to think about it.

—Kathleen Dowling Singh

Contemplation calls that ordinary mind into question and says that this thing we call *thinking* cannot get us there. We need a different operating system, and it begins with silence and leads to silence.

In my book *The Naked Now*, I called non-silence "dualistic thinking," where everything is separated into opposites, such as life and death. The dualistic mind is almost the only mind left in the West. We even think that this is what it means to be educated—to be very good at dualistic thinking—but it is what Jesus and Buddha would call judgmental thinking (see Matthew 7:1–5), and they both strongly warn against it.

Dualistic thinking is operative almost all of the time. It occurs when we choose one side or temperamentally prefer one side, and then we call the other side false, wrong, heretical, or untrue. The other side is often something to which we have not yet been exposed, or it threatens us or our ego in some way, or it is beyond our education. The dualistic mind splits the moment and forbids the dark side, the mysterious, and the paradoxical. This is the common level of conversation that we have in the world. Basically, it lacks humility and patience, and it is the opposite of contemplation.

Nondual thinking is precisely contemplation. It is not a very inspiring term for what many think of as prayer, but it is a clinically descriptive word of exactly what is happening. The Holy Spirit frees us from taking sides and allows us to remain content in the partial darkness of every situation long enough to let it teach us, broaden us, and enrich us. We have to practice for many years, and make many mistakes in the meantime, to learn how to do this. Paul beautifully speaks of it in Philippians 4:6–7: "Pray with gratitude and the peace of Christ, which is beyond knowledge or understanding ['the making of distinctions'], will guard both your mind and your heart in Christ Jesus." It is all right there in concise form. Teachers of contemplation teach us how to stand guard and not let our emotions and obsessive thoughts control us.

When we are thinking nondualistically, with this guarded mind and heart, we will feel poor for a moment, and we will also be stunned into an embarrassing silence.

THE HISTORY OF NONDUALISM

In the Christian tradition, nondualism stood the test of time for fifteen hundred years. Certainly, *The Cloud of Unknowing*, a fourteenth-century Middle English Christian mystical guide to contemplation, made clear that nondualism was still very much a part of the Christian tradition. Knowing had to be balanced by unknowing, and saying balanced by not saying. Its underlying message was that the only way to truly know God is to abandon all preconceived notions and beliefs or knowledge about God and surrender to unknowingness, at which point we begin to glimpse the true nature of God.

This tradition of not knowing, which is sometimes called the *apophatic* way, had been a central part of Christian teaching since Dionysius the Pseudo-Areopagite in the late sixth century, whom even the Scholastic theologians Thomas Aquinas (1225–1274) and Bonaventure (1221–1274) still extensively referenced seven centuries later.

When we put knowing together with not knowing, and even become willing not to know, we have this marvelous phenomenon called *faith*, which allows us to keep an open horizon, an open field. We can thus remain in a humble and wondrous beginner's mind, even as we grow older—and maybe even more so.

Today, scientists seem to do this better than many Christian clergy. Those in the scientific community can live with a working hypothesis, can move forward with theory, while too many in the religious community need to have the whole truth *right now* and in clear and certain words: "My denomination has the whole truth; your denomination/religion does not." What a waste of time. Can't we see that those words demonstrate a love of self even more than a love of truth? We developed this style after the Reformation, when Europe divided into Catholics and Lutherans. Each group had to prove that it was 100 percent right, and the other group was 100 percent wrong—which was and is, of course, never true.

Then, right on the heels of the Reformation, we had this strangely named phenomenon of the Enlightenment. They stole *our* word! Did you ever think of that? That was a Christian Scripture concept, largely emerging from Jesus, who said that he was the Enlightener (John 8:12) and we would share in that enlightenment (see John 9; Matthew 5:14–16). How did such a broad and spiritual term come to mean being merely rational? We lost our own unique and brilliant way of knowing as we tried to imitate our antagonists and borrowed their very limited vocabulary and perspective.

Rationality is a fine mode of thinking. It produced the Industrial Revolution, the Scientific Revolution, the Mechanical Revolution, and the Medical Revolution. Most of us would not be alive without it right now, so thank God for the dualistic, rational mind. It is good, as far as it goes, but it cannot go far enough. There is a ceiling above which the rational mind cannot go.

I would suggest that there are six issues that the rational mind cannot process or explain: love, sex, death, life itself, suffering, and infinity. What ever made us think that the truly great things were simply rational? When we limit our understanding of these issues to a rational level, we block our openness to the non-rational ways of perceiving: our emotional intelligence, the intuitive, the personal, and the contextual—all of which are necessary to know something spiritually or fully. We have tried to resolve crucial issues with dualistic morality, dogmas, and doctrines, using low-level consciousness, and thus we cannot reach the higher levels of consciousness or mystical experience.

One of the reasons I accepted the invitation to speak at the Festival of Faiths was because, a few miles down the road at the Abbey of Gethsemani, Thomas Merton had almost single-handedly pulled back the veil and reintroduced the word *contemplation* to a Roman Catholic Church that no longer understood it and to a Protestant era that was never taught the concept at all. Thank God, there were many exceptions: people who came to a contemplative mind on their own, through great love and great suffering, without ever knowing that they were contemplatives or using the word to describe themselves. We are living in a marvelous time today, a time when the contemplative mind is being rediscovered.

After the Reformation and the Enlightenment, the Roman Catholic Church circled the wagons into a little defensive shell. We called it a "siege mentality." Each of the other Christian denominations did the same. We each lusted after certitude, order, and explanations to prove that our denomination was right, as if that were faith—or love. We didn't realize that much of the world would look at us and conclude that our whole religion was wrong if it could waste time on such egocentric fighting! For the most part, contemplation was no longer systematically taught, even in the religious orders and within contemplative communities, as Thomas Merton had prophetically told his brothers.

Yet there are many people whose souls still live in that silent, spacious, open place, and this is invariably the fruit of great love or great suffering, and usually both.[1]

This is the natural and universally available path to contemplation for all people. You do not need to be celibate, monastic, or even especially ascetical (except in your mind and heart) to be a contemplative.

Although the universally available paths are love and great suffering, conscious inner prayer will accelerate the path to contemplation and transformation. But the mere reciting of prayers can also be, as St. John Cassian (360–435) called it, a *pax perniciosa*, a "dangerous peace." This early Christian monk, who brought the ideas and practices of Egyptian monasticism to the early medieval West, saw that even the way of prayer can be dangerous if it never leads us to great love and allows us to avoid necessary suffering in the name of religion.

Those who fall into the safety net of silence find that it is not at all a descent into individualism. In fact, if it is individualistic, it is that dangerous peace. True prayer or contemplation is instead a leap into commonality and community. We know that what we are experiencing is held by the whole and that we are not alone anymore. We are a part, and forever a grateful part.

That is why people can, if they are called to it, be celibate, because they live in a kind of intimacy with everything. Everything is a jolt, a joy, a possibility, a communion, a connection. In fact, celibacy is wrong for anybody to choose if they have not moved to some level of contemplative prayer because celibacy is not going to work without prayer, and they will end up as fruitless and frustrated bachelors and spinsters. That is also one reason why the Roman Catholic Church has had the pedophilia scandals. Well-intentioned young boys went off to seminaries, thinking they could live life at this deeper level, but they did not have the inner tools to know how to do it.

On a lesser level, the church did the same thing to the laity by telling them to believe doctrines such as those of the Trinity or the two natures of Christ, neither of which can be understood with a dualistic mind. All the laity can do is intellectually assent to such doctrines, which have no dynamic possibility in the soul. Doctrines cannot open up your heart or mind or give you foundational peace. In fact, they close off your heart and mind because you are living in a kind of unreality.

The principle of three, which we call Trinity, undoes the principle of two, and it declares that all the power is in the relationships between the entities. As the theologian, Episcopal priest, writer, and retreat leader Cynthia Bourgeault states, "The whole important thing about the doctrine of the Trinity is [that] all the power is not in the names of the three particles, but in the relationship between."[2]

There is a foundational pattern of giving and receiving in every aspect of the universe—modeled on the very shape of God as Trinity. Once we have a dynamic waterwheel of outflowing love, as St. Bonaventure called it, it flows in only one direction: always positive, always giving, always outpouring, where there is no possibility of anger, unlove, wrath, or hatred in God.

The doctrine of the Trinity was developed to order to move us to the dynamic principle of three, where there is always movement forward. But the ego naturally pulls us back into the principle of two, which is inherently comparative, competitive, and antagonistic, and usually either/or. Trinity undoes that. All we can do is jump into the flow and allow it to happen. The only way of really jumping in is through standing in love—even in our mind. An aphorism I often use is this:

> Watch your thoughts; they become words.
> Watch your words; they become actions.
> Watch your actions; they become habits.
> Watch your habits; they become your character.
> Watch your character; it becomes your destiny.

Contemplation and silence nip the ego and its negatives in the bud by teaching us how to watch and guard our very thoughts.

Solitude Versus Silence

I want to make an important distinction between solitude and silence. Solitude, of itself, is not silence. Solitude perhaps emerges because we do not like people, or we are angry at others, or we want to get away from noisy people, or we are introverted—and there is nothing inherently wrong or right about that. But there is nothing transformative about this kind of solitude. It is running, which is the opposite of connecting.

A true solitude has to fall into a larger silence, a shared silence, something far beyond the absence of noise. True silence holds the contraries in a way that words cannot. It mediates and resolves the polarities from each side. Silence is the space in between words and around ideas. Each side of every argument must travel over the broad, appeasing surface of silence before it can reach the other side. When walking over that broad road of silence, we are much humbler and less judgmental. Silence also does not put words into the mouth of the other or make caricatures of the other side. It certainly does not call names, but patiently waits for the other to fully name themselves.

Without that silence around words and ideas, we only have more analysis and endless commentary. This is what we cease to do in contemplative practice. We stop the commentary, especially once we realize how self-referential most of it is. Such inner dialogues will never get us anywhere close to Great Truth.

We all have rehearsed an upcoming argument in our heads, whether it is with a boss, a spouse, or someone close to us. It's just like the prodigal son returning home, practicing what he is going to say to Dad (see Luke 15:11–32). The fearful ego practices its defensive posture.

But when we do that, we use the words that we think are going to win our case, to defeat the other side. We are not, if we are honest with ourselves, really searching for truth, but rather working to look good, to look right, to keep the job, to keep our marriage, or whatever it might be—and God surely understands that.

But the contemplative mind moves beyond that level to read reality from a different perspective than either/or. We named one of my books *Yes, And…* rather than *Yes, But* because the "but" makes the phrase contrary: this, not that. It sets us up for antagonistic or defensive thinking.

As a Roman Catholic priest, I am trained in the tradition. I know the tradition and I know orthodoxy. But we Franciscans often think of ourselves as having an alternative orthodoxy inside the Roman Catholic Church, emphasizing different things. In general, Francis emphasized *orthopraxy* over mere verbal orthodoxy, focusing on how we live over what we say we believe. We are now seeing the same emphasis in his namesake, Pope Francis, and it is setting the world on fire.

St. Francis was not an academic. He emphasized living a simple, nonviolent life in this world. The line attributed to him that is popular today is actually a paraphrase of something he put in our Franciscan Rule and in one of his "Admonitions": "Preach the gospel at all times. When necessary, use words." He also says similar things to the friars as recorded in his earliest biographies.

Preach the gospel at all times. Lifestyle was itself the gospel, the emphasis—similar to the traditions of the Mennonites, Amish, Waldensians, and Quakers. Let's not argue about words because such arguments always lead to the dualistic taking of sides. Let's just live in a way that shouts, "Jesus!" Live in a way that exudes the love and compassion of Jesus.

Silence, of course, is not fighting about any doctrine, but agreeing to not fully know and not speak too quickly. It is a way of life more than an imposed doctrine. Inside of silence—especially extended silence—we see that things find their true order and meaning somewhat naturally. When things find their true order, we know what is important, what lasts, what is real, and what Jesus would call the Kingdom or Reign of God—in other words, the big stuff. All the rest is passing. All those things you were emotional about last Wednesday that you cannot even remember are what the Buddhists rightly call emptiness. They have no lasting substance. In that sense, they are not real.

Yet we give our lives for emotions that are over and gone by next week. We wrap our egos around them and give them a weight and importance they do not deserve. Feelings are inherently self-referential: they help us know ourselves but also keep us in our own little world if we take them too seriously or attach to them. Feelings are, first of all, always about "me," which give us good self-knowledge but also trap us in ourselves if we do not use them to go further.

My metaphor for Jesus' Reign of God is simply the Big Picture. In the Big Picture, what matters? When you are on your deathbed, what will matter? Will you be thinking about what you are thinking about now? Will you be arguing about what you are arguing about now? To pull back from the tug of emotion and the ego that wants to be right, wants to win, wants to put the other down, and wants to humiliate the enemy is the very heart of spiritual warfare. This is where we need to put our energy first, instead of obsessing about theoretical or real moral issues that usually ask little of us personally.

There is something we find so sweet about taking sides, about feeling that we've made our case. But silence allows things to emerge in their wholeness—as Ken Wilber would say, "all levels, all stages" of growth[3]—instead of our usual state of being trapped at one level, one stage.

At that one level, that one stage, we each make our case. That is why all arguments between people at different levels of growth are doomed to some degree of misunderstanding. Outside the contemplative mind, those arguments are almost always egocentric and about winning. Our United States Congress has made this overwhelmingly clear in recent years, as our otherwise educated representatives speak so narrowly and blindly that we now expect it of them. Such a level of conversation is not about love or the pursuit of truth as such, or even about reality. It is about the love of victory, which is pretty much all that the ego wants, along with making sure that the other side loses.

The dualistic mind loves to exaggerate the differences— anything that can be considered a defect in the other person. When we have not experienced communion, when we have not experienced unitive consciousness, all we have left are our differences. They become an easy reference point, and we choose to overplay them. Focusing on differences forms the early stages of what René Girard (1923–2015) rightly called "the scapegoat mechanism," which he believed largely operates unconsciously. Contemplation is about making us conscious of such things.

In the first half of life, we are all rather dualistic and truly need to start there. We need to first make distinctions before we can then move beyond them. We expect young people to make distinctions and focus on winning. They know their group, their team, their nationality, their race, their religion, and their neighborhood. Most of history has been in a first-half-of-life consciousness up to now.

Most people never had time for, or a model of, the second half of life, which is no longer about winning, but rather about being and having inner integrity. Silence makes space for that larger and truer level of being, if we allow it to.

We need to see silence, and nothingness itself, as a kind of being in the great chain of being, perhaps the first link from which all others emerge. St. Bonaventure, the Italian spiritual genius who picked up the intellectual thread from the non-academic Francis, led us through the great chain of being, from material things to inner soul, and then to the Divine. John Duns Scotus (1266–1308), another early Franciscan, taught that we may speak of being with one voice: from the being of the earth itself, to the waters upon the earth, to the minerals within the earth, to the flowers and trees and grasses, then the animals, the humans, the angelic choirs, and the Divine.

Both of these mystics would have said that once we stop seeing the Divine in any link of that chain, the whole thing will fall apart. It is either all God's work, or we will have a hard time finding God in each part. That split and confused world is the postmodern world we live in today, which no longer knows how to surround and ground all things in silence.

This is not an oversimplification. Either we see God in all things, or very quickly we cannot see God anywhere, even in our own species. Yet we Christians have spent the five hundred years since the Reformation dividing and deciding where God was, believing God was in our church but not in yours. Interestingly enough, we determined it was usually "my church" that God preferred and where God resided. It was the very lie that Jesus tried to undo among his own chosen people, and he experienced the same backlash.

Even in the old *Baltimore Catechism*, taught to generations of American Catholic young people, the Church gave mixed messages about God. The answer to question 15, "Where is God?" was "God is everywhere." But, throughout the rest of the catechism, we learned that God really is not everywhere, but only in the Roman Catholic Church. And in the Roman Catholic Church, Jesus is only in the tabernacle. And that was only if the priest celebrated a valid Mass and was in the state of grace. Thus, God was locked up, and only the priest possessed the key. We unwittingly laid a foundation for modern atheism because we kept saying where God was not, and where God was not even allowed to be. Immature Christianity actually gave birth to secularism by not appreciating the silence, the beauty, and the grace that connect everything with everything else in the universe. We did this by not honoring the humble silence that precedes all our words and distinctions.

While claiming on the one hand that God is everywhere, we asserted, in effect, that God is hardly anywhere.

Silence allows the whole to exist and does not get lost in and over-identify with the parts. Without silence, almost all things become boring, superfluous, or just another thing, and we become preoccupied with size, mass, speed, influence, and celebrities rather than with meaning or significance. It seems that only poets and mystics now have time for meaning or depth.

Silence is that ever-faithful companion, a portal to a constantly deeper connection with whatever is in front of us. That which is in front of us does not need to be big or important. It can be a stone. It can be a grasshopper. Anything can convert us once we surround it with this reverent silence that gives it significance, identity, singularity, importance, and value, or what Scotus called the "thisness" of everything.

Scotus, building again on Francis' love of animals and creation—Brother Sun, Sister Moon—taught that God does not create genus and species. God only creates *this*: this frog, this moment, this dog. The fact that *this* dog is persisting and being in *this* moment means that God is choosing it and loving it right now or it would fall into oblivion. That is good!

There is only *thisness* in good Franciscan philosophy, which is another way of speaking of the mystery of incarnation. It is why so many poets liked John Duns Scotus. English poet and Jesuit priest Gerard Manley Hopkins (1844–1889) was a Scotist, as was American Trappist monk and mystic Thomas Merton. The Jesuit priest and scientist Pierre Teilhard de Chardin (1881–1955) would be Scotus' modern counterpart in Tellhard's love of material and concrete things.

Conclusion

Silence is a dwelling place that is at once horizontal, allowing connection with the thisness, the singularity of everything, but it is also, at the same time, vertical. It allows us to find, through those things, doorways to the eternal. Silence takes away the noise we project onto everything and allows individual things to stand in, stand for, and even stand apart so that we can see the light and life that they reveal. *This* is always the doorway to *that*—and to more. The one is the window by which we can see the many. If it is true here, it soon becomes true everywhere.

Silence attracts meaning. If we stay silent for a whole hour, it will be hard not to write a poem. In silence, everything becomes real. Everything deserves a poem. Silence discloses the fullness of the now, instead of always waiting and wanting more, instead of waiting for the next thing, the more exciting thing, to happen.

We have to remember that *how we do anything is how we do everything*. How we do this moment is how we are going to do the next moment. If we're bored to death with this moment, we're going to be bored to death with the next moment.

We have to be awake *right now*, and we can be awake through silence. It is not a matter of being more moral but of being more conscious—which will eventually make us much more moral.

What it means to be vulnerable before a moment is to give it the power to change us. If we do not give another person, animal, event, situation, or emotion the power to influence us, to change us, then we are not intimate with the moment, not vulnerable before the only reality we have.

In many ways, intimacy before the moment, vulnerability in the presence of all reality, is the very definition of spirituality. It would indeed be heroic if we could live our whole life inside of this kind of semi-permeable membrane. It would allow all events in, enough to really change us, and allow us out of our prisons— to change the world a bit, I would hope. If our spirituality does not make us more vulnerable, I doubt whether it is much good.

If we respond to a little bit of silence, it seems to hide. But if we remain open, then it reveals more. It reveals and hides, reveals and hides, reveals and hides. It waits to see if we are going to use it in a non-manipulative way. If we remain non-manipulative, it gives even more of itself. Please think about that for a while.

So be patient with silence. It gives a little, and then it gives more if we do not abuse the initial silence. It is like floating in water; once we stop fighting it, we float even better.

Leave the silence open-ended. Do not try to settle the dust. Do not rush to resolve the inner conflict. Do not seek a glib, quick answer, but leave all things for a while in the silent space. Do not rush to judgment. That is what it really means that God alone is the judge (see James 4:12). Inner silence frees us from the burden of thinking that our judgment is needed or important.

Real silence moves us from knowing things to perceiving a presence that has a reality in itself. Could that be God? There is then a mutuality between each of us and all things. There is an I-Thou relationship, as twentieth-century Austrian-Israeli Jewish philosopher Martin Buber (1878–1965) would call it. He wrote that an I-It (*Ich-Es*) relationship is when we experience everything as a commodity, as useful, as utilitarian. But the I-Thou (*Ich-Du*) relationship is when we can simply respect a thing as it is without adjusting it, naming it, changing it, fixing it, controlling it, or trying to explain it. Is that the mind that can know God? I really think so.

Such silence is the peace the world cannot give (John 14:27). That does not mean that there is not a place for explaining, not a place for understanding, but we first have to learn to say yes to the moment. *Yes* is where we have to begin. If we start with no, which is critiquing, judging, pigeonholing, analyzing, and dismissing, it is very hard to get back to yes.

We must learn to start every single encounter with a foundational yes, before we ever dare to move to no. That is the heart of contemplation, and it takes a lifetime of practice. You have now begun and can live each day with a forever-returning beginner's mind. It will always be silent before it dares to speak.

CHAPTER TWO

Sacred Silence: Pathway to Compassion

GOD AS FLOW

It is strange to me that Christianity, the religion that believes the Word became flesh, has become so wordy that much of its history involves fighting about words, using words in different ways, defining words, and defending words. We reversed the incarnational process of God and made the flesh become word again (but no longer the Eternal Word!).

You would think that we would have been much more concerned about what we call *incarnation*, the enfleshment, the physical world, if we believed what we said we believe: that God became incarnate in this Jewish man called Jesus. That is the belief of the Christian tradition. But our history has been quite Gnostic, if we are honest, more like *excarnation* than incarnation, invariably preferring theory over practice.

Something supremely orthodox in the Christian tradition is the doctrine of the Trinity. The shape of God in orthodox Christian belief is that God is more a verb than a noun. God is a relationship. God is a communion among those we call Father, Son, and Holy Spirit. We gave them masculine names, although we always argue about whether the Holy Spirit is feminine.

But as theologian Cynthia Bourgeault says, even in that composition, women still lose: there are the Father and the Son, and it is still two to one. She urges us not to argue about whether the figures of the Trinity are all masculine or all feminine, as that misses the point. The important thing to focus on is the relationship among them, not the precise names or genders of the three persons.[1]

What happened is that we isolated who we believed was the Incarnate One, the Visible One, the Christ, from this process of communion, of mutual outpouring, which words prove inadequate to describe and which cannot be talked about. The doctrine of the Trinity could have given us much more patience with silence and mystery, but we wanted something to talk about. So the Visible One, Christ Jesus, became the One we mostly talked about. We pretty much treated Jesus as God and forgot that the Trinity was God, which significantly rearranged the Christian mind and made mysticism much rarer and even mistrusted.

To put it very honestly, we Christians overplayed the Jesus card. We pulled Jesus out of this dynamic union of the Trinity. Then we pushed Jesus, for all practical purposes, into the God role, when his role was much different—it was to put God and humanity into one! We did not know how to put it together in him, and the sad result was that we had no model or suggestion that we could also put the two together in ourselves.

Let us look at our first attempts at language to describe the indescribable, though we might use different vocabulary today. Our use of masculine words is, at least in part, a historical accident, with the use of the word *Father* to describe God as the Creator and Source. Jesus himself described his God as *Abba*, Father—actually, "Daddy"—and this was very helpful in a world where the male was usually patriarchal, mistrusted, and surely not a loving daddy. Jesus calling God *Abba* began the needed healing, but, unfortunately, we took the metaphor literally, which has created a lot of pushback and negative projection over time. God the Father ended up looking like another patriarch instead of letting the Trinitarian flow redefine the very notion of patriarchy itself (which I hope will become clear through this teaching) or learning to relate to this Father the way that Jesus did.

Christians believe the doctrine of the Trinity is the absolute foundational theology of Christianity. Yet in the early 1960s, German Jesuit Karl Rahner (1904–1984) wrote, "Should the doctrine of the Trinity have to be dropped as false, the major part of religious literature could well remain virtually unchanged."[2] How could this be true? It is not bad will or even bad theology, but we simply lacked the inner tools to deal with it. The doctrine of the Trinity invites and, in fact, necessitates nondual consciousness. We need a contemplative mind to even begin to process this nonrational mystery of God.

Other religions do not have to accept the Christian vocabulary and the Christian metaphor of the Trinity. But while we use different language, most religions, at the mature levels, have come to a notion of God as a dynamic flow, a communion, relationship itself, or the very "ground of being" as Paul wrote (Acts 17:28).

This Father God, whom our Jewish ancestors had discovered and reverenced, was, first of all, beyond words. God's name—Yahweh—could not be spoken (see Exodus 3:14 and 20:7). To use this name was to use it "in vain." The message was, "You do not know what you are talking about when you use the word *God*."[3] Any word is in vain, and yet some word must be spoken. Our Jewish ancestors gave us a marvelous sense of humility before God and Yahweh's ineffability.

With the use of the wonderful metaphor "Father" (remember that nothing besides metaphor is possible for God), Christian belief in the Formless One took form because we humans had to picture One whom we could love and to whom we could relate (1 John 1:1–2). We had to start with a healing metaphor to begin a trustful relationship. The trouble arose when we took the metaphor literally and thought that God was actually of the human male gender. It's rather silly when you think of it, but at least it was a start.

The one Christians call the Holy Spirit was precisely the love relationship between Father and Son, which again could not be named or perfectly described. The Holy Spirit is the "Third Something" that takes on a reality and life of its own, like the love relationship between partners. The best we could do was to come up with further metaphors, like descending dove, fire, wind, and flowing water—all dynamic words and helpful symbols to describe the active and living relationship, the inner movements that we call the Indwelling Holy Spirit.

We forget too often that the only possible languages of religion are metaphor and simile. It comes as a great shock to most Christians that every word we use is metaphor or simile: it is *like*, it is *like*, it is *like*. If we as a Christian community would have been more honest and accepted the Jewish commandment that any name for God is in vain and is not a perfect or even adequate description, we would have developed much more humility around words—and around religion itself. Even now, many Roman Catholics look for mystery through incense and Latin instead of resting in and struggling with the foundational mystery itself.

We are called to honor the Father, the Holy Spirit, and the One who took human shape and identity, and the relationship among them, instead of just focusing on Jesus, which became the

Christian religion in its most common forms. It is that overemphasis on Jesus—and less on relationship—which also had the consequence of setting us in competition with the other world religions. We have to prove Jesus all the time, in contradistinction to the Buddha, Allah, Hindu gods, or even the God of Israel. In doing so, we pulled the Christ out of the very union about which he talked, that he enjoyed, and into which he invited us. An honest Trinitarianism actually opens up interfaith dialogue and respect, because now we can admit that God is also total mystery and inner aliveness, rather than a Jesus standing apart from these.

That is the irony of it: we ended up not being faithful to our own tradition by overemphasizing merely one part of it. We prayed to Christ instead of, as the official prayers still state, "through Christ our Lord." We forgot the shape of God and how we were a part of that shape as the "body of Christ." What an enormous loss.

When we overplayed the Jesus card and made Jesus into the founder of our new religion, we forgot that he died as a faithful Jew. He did not know that he was founding the Christian religion in his human mind (which is rather clear from the Gospels, if we are honest about them). Instead, he was trying to reform his own faith tradition—and all religion—to address its idolatries. I surely hope Catholics know that he never heard of the Roman Catholic Church—or any other church, for that matter. He went to the synagogue and temple. This is shocking for us, I suppose, but a necessary shock.

THE TANGENT OF HISTORY

We have to recognize that we understood our Christian religion outside of any honest historical context. What happened very quickly was that we not only became separated from our roots in Judaism, but we also aligned ourselves with the Roman Empire after 313 BCE. Then, we collaborated with power, war, and money in Europe, largely until the second half of the twentieth century, when the two world wars revealed the whole mismatch for all the world to see.

While that confluence of events had some good aspects—I am not saying it was all bad—our alignment with the Roman Empire, the Holy Roman Empire, the Spanish Monarchy, and the British Empire made it necessary again and again to defend and to prove that our God was better than other gods. Empires need an agreed-upon god to hold together, and it does not matter if we actually follow this god's teachings. This humble Jewish man—Jesus—became a theocratic figure. The Incarnate One became the Transcendent Judge. He became the *Pantocrator* (Omnipotent and Wrathful Lord of the Universe), which has almost no basis in Scripture. Compare that to the simple early drawings of the Good Shepherd and the "Crucified Ass" (or *Alexamenos graffito*, scratched into plaster in Rome and now located in the Palatine Museum). These drawings are entirely different from the imperial images of Jesus that profoundly influenced and continue to influence Christian practice to this day.

Deus, the Latin word for God, is really a form of the Greek word Zeus. We were basically dealing with a pagan notion of god, which became Jesus, who soon had hardly anything to do with the historical Jesus. Instead, he was the available and needed god figure that held the whole Roman Empire together. In fact, some art historians teach that the Christ *Pantocrator* image which took over Christian basilicas after the fourth century is a precise attempt to imitate the foreboding image of Zeus (Jove or Jupiter) in Greek and Roman temples. Aa a crucified loser, Jesus was not an image with which an empire or the ego was comfortable—or ever could be.

Yet there were always people who went to the deeper level, what I call the underground stream, where the unspeakable, the mystery, was still honored and allowed. But, by and large, we moved from our position as the immoral minority to the seemingly moral majority, and that radically shifted our vantage point.

The deeper and older stream can be found, of course, in John's Gospel and many of Paul's teachings, then later in the Desert Fathers and Mothers, and soon the concept moved into Egypt, Syria, Cappadocia in eastern Turkey, and areas of Palestine. This is where the mystical tradition first developed, and where the contemplative life was discovered and taught, revealing that we needed a different mind to comprehend such high-level teaching. They did not fight about doctrines, but instead about the best ways to find inner quiet. Try to feel the radical difference that makes. Read the *Philokalia*, a collection of fourth- through fifteenth-century texts from the Eastern Orthodox Church if you want to know this for yourself.

These early Christian mystics were able to demonstrate and teach that the normal, early stage dualistic mind cannot "understand spiritual things in a spiritual way" (1 Corinthians 2:13). It is too weak an instrument to understand what it might mean when Jesus says, "the Father and I are one" (John 10:30): that they are actually sharing with us this same Spirit and inviting us into their relationship.

We cannot understand this new principle of three using the old dualistic principle of two, which is always an antagonistic, either/or, right-or-wrong kind of thinking. This dualistic thinking continued in Roman Catholicism throughout the centuries and did much to create the two-level Christianity (clerics/religious versus laity) against which Martin Luther (1483–1546) rightly reacted.

Monks, friars, and nuns, while not all contemplatives, formed the heart of every religious community (like my own Franciscan community) and were responsible for the rediscovery of the contemplative mind in our time. Thomas Merton led the charge into the past and back into our future. So many of the early religious became hermits because they could not survive in the commonly dualistic religious life. Many lay people, through great love and great suffering, became "hidden contemplatives," but usually with little support from the clergy, so they also stepped out of mainstream religion to survive.

Whenever we see a recurrence of hermits, anchorites, recluses, and hermitages, we can know that such an age has rediscovered nondual or contemplative thinking. We cannot endure silence and solitude for long with a dualistic mind. We will drive ourselves crazy with inner arguments.

Unfortunately, however, this splitting off did create a two-level society, and the average Roman Catholic in the average church in Florence or Heidelberg or Boston really was not expected to learn the contemplative mind. They were just taught to pay, pray, and obey. Their praying did not really mean contemplative prayer, but rather the saying of scripted prayers or the social prayer of liturgy, where they could know if they were doing it right or wrong, which is a strong ego need. Unfortunately, there is little call to honest shadow work, humility, or mystery at this level. It is mostly about conforming to the group.

The marvel of living in our time is that this tradition of contemplation is being retrieved and named honestly again. Yes, we had it, and we lost it, but we continually rediscover it. Up to now, it has been marginalized somewhere off to the edge so that it was not expected from or offered to the ordinary Christian believer— or the ordinary clergy who did all the preaching and teaching. That is fundamentally why Roman Catholicism split into at least three major levels: the clergy, who held it all together; the laity, who did what the clergy told them to do; and the monks, nuns, and friars who, in effect, moved off to the side of the tradition to find the old depth—with varying degrees of success, of course.

Thank God for the Protestant Reformation in the sixteenth century, because, up to that point, we Roman Catholics were the only game in town. We had a monopoly on supposed Christianity, at least in the West. There was no loyal opposition to keep Christianity somewhat on target, or even honest, especially since we had lost almost all contact with the Eastern Church after the Great Schism of 1054. We learned again and again that absolute power corrupts absolutely.

Without prophetic thinking—that is, self-critical thinking, which we originally learned from the Jews—all religion becomes idolatrous and self-serving. The Reformation tried to reform, but it did not largely result in a recovery of the contemplative tradition. Instead, Christianity became even more heady, more verbal, and more argumentative than it had been before. This was accompanied by the invention of the printing press, which had the side effect of moving us largely into the left brain, with both good and bad forms of rational thinking.

It had to happen. We had to go through it, but now we are at the end of five centuries of endless Christian argumentation. The world is tired of it and does not listen anymore. The historical issues over which we divided are not even interesting to most people, inside or outside of Christianity. It is surely hard for outsiders to take us seriously, since each group claims it is the only one that Jesus loves, the only one that is following him correctly. We reveal little of the mystical, dynamic, Trinitarian flow of life among us, within us, or toward others.

Naturally and rightfully, we Christians find ourselves in a very defensive position today because the secular West says, "Show us the fruit; show us the future." Where did the two world wars come from? They did not come from "pagan" Asia, as we thought of it, but the little continent that we Christians thought we had in the bag. We were all Catholics and Christians in that little part of the world called Europe, and yet that is where world wars started. That is where the Holocaust happened. That is where people across a continent formed by the Christian tradition slaughtered one another twice in one century. Europe's preferences and colonies are perhaps the most materialistic in the world to this day. "What happened to Jesus as their ideal and teacher?" the world must be asking.

The centuries of anti-Semitism in most parts of Europe that laid the ground for the Holocaust were ironically like killing our grandparents. When we separate from our grandparents—which is our Jewish heritage—and we do not even know that they are our grandparents, we end up killing the very ones we should honor and love. It is cultural schizophrenia, and it will stand forever as a massive judgment on the immaturity of Western Christianity and our amazing capacity for missing the point. It is also a final bad fruit of dualistic thinking—which insists on an enemy, a scapegoat onto whom we can dump our own untransformed evil.

When we lose the contemplative mind, or nondual consciousness, we invariably create violent people. The dualistic mind is endlessly argumentative, and we created an argumentative continent, which we also exported to the Americas. We see it in our politics. We see it in the church's inability to create much sincere interfaith dialogue—or even intra-faith dialogue. The Baptists are still fighting the Anglicans as "lost" and the Evangelicals are dismissing the Catholics as the "Whore of Babylon," and we Catholics are demeaning everybody else as heretics, and each of us is hiding in our small, smug circles. What a waste of time and good God-energy, while the world suffers and declines. We have divided Jesus.

Simone Weil (1909–1943), the marvelous French philosopher and political activist, stood on the edge of Christianity and

Judaism her whole life, wanting her very life to be a bridge—
loving both traditions and not being able to choose either of
them. Her great message was that the trouble with Christianity
is that it had made itself into a separate religion instead of recog-
nizing that the prophetic message of Jesus might just be necessary
for the reform and authenticity of all religions.

But Christians made Christianity into a competition, and once
we were in competition, we had to be largely verbal. Soon, we
were aggressive and, saddest of all, we became quite violent—all
in the name of God. One follows from the other, and unless
we nip it in the bud of thoughts and feelings—which is what
contemplative prayer does—our thoughts invariably become
words, our words become actions, our actions become habits,
our habits become our character, and our character becomes our
final destiny.

Because I was lucky enough to be exposed to it as a Franciscan,
I cannot doubt or deny that the deeper stream of contemplation
was always there. It was never the mainstream, and I have to be
honest about that now. It was relegated to a minority position.
Even today, when I tell most Christians about contemplation, it
can sound heretical, new, or unnecessary.

When we know the Judeo-Christian perennial tradition, and
we discover the deeper stream, it is just so easy to communicate
effectively with members of other faith traditions. We can talk
from a common base. I was trained in Roman Catholic orthodox

traditional theology, and that very Judeo-Christian tradition, at the contemplative level, taught me to honor the visibility and revelation of God in all the world traditions. What a paradox—but not really at all. When we go deep in one place, we invariably fall into the deep and common underground stream.

The intention of our Living School in Albuquerque, New Mexico is to reintroduce the West to the underground stream of perennial tradition that we all share. That does not mean that I encourage you to abandon your own mother tradition. We have to know the rules before we can know when and how to properly break the rules. We have to be surrendered and accountable to one tradition, as both the Dalai Lama and Mother Teresa (1910–1997) have insisted. Otherwise, our ego self is always the decider, and we operate outside the living Body of Christ.

In that deeper underground stream, silence is much more possible because we know that all words are inadequate anyway. All words are faulty. All words are "yes, and." I think if we could surround our religions with that kind of humility, with that kind of patience, we all would find this conversation entirely easy and natural.

CHAPTER THREE

The True Self Is Compassion, Love Itself

For Christians who have gone to their own depths—which is not all of us, unfortunately—there is the uncovering of an indwelling Presence, which might even be experienced as Martin Buber's "I-Thou" relationship. It is a deep and loving yes that is inherent within us. In Christian theology, this inner Presence is described as the Holy Spirit, which is precisely God as immanent, within our being, and our deepest and truest self.

Some saints and mystics have described this Presence as "closer to me than I am to myself" or "more me than I am myself." Many of us would also describe this, as Thomas Merton did, as the True Self. Yet, it still must be awakened and chosen. The Holy Spirit is totally given and given equally to all, but it must be received too. One who totally receives this Presence and draws life from it is what we call a saint.

That is how "image" becomes "likeness," to use those important two words in the creation of humans (Genesis 1:26–27). We all have the indwelling image, but we surrender to the likeness in varying degrees and stages. None of us is morally or psychologically perfect or whole, but saints and mystics nevertheless dare to believe that they are ontologically ("in their very being") whole. That is totally a gift from God. It has nothing to do with "me."

The Holy Spirit is never created by our actions or behavior. It is naturally indwelling, our *inner being* with God. In Roman Catholic theology, we call the Holy Spirit "Uncreated Grace." Culture and even religion often teach us to live out of our false self: reputation, self-image, role, possessions, money, appearance, and so on. It is only as this false self fails us, and it always eventually does, that the True Self stands revealed and ready to guide us. Some enlightened souls surrender to this truth and presence much earlier than others.

The True Self does not teach us compassion as much as it *is* compassion already. From this more spacious and grounded place, we naturally connect, empathize, forgive, and love just about everything. We were made in love, for love, and unto love. (We now have scientific and biological evidence for this, as we see that our neo-mammalian brain holds positive emotions of contentment and desire to nurture. We can see it operating naturally in all mammals as they live in their roles peacefully, feed and protect their young, and seem to accept the inevitability of suffering and death much more naturally than humans do with our fancy neocortex—which wants to fix and explain everything.)

This deep inner yes is God in me, already loving God through me. The false self does not really know how to love in a very deep or broad way. It is too opportunistic. It is too small. It is too self-referential to be compassionate.

The True Self—in which you and God are one—does not choose to love as much as it *is* love itself already (see Colossians 3:3–4). Loving from this vast space is experienced as a river within you that flows of its own accord (see John 7:38–39).

CHAPTER FOUR

Looking Out in Prayer with Contemplative Eyes

To speak of mysticism in simple terms means to speak of experiential knowledge of God instead of merely mental or cognitive knowledge of God. When we really experience the Divine, we naturally move to a higher (or deeper) level of consciousness. When most people hear the word *mystical*, they think it means something impossible for most of us or only available to those who have been ascetical for twenty-five years. However, mystical encounters come to people who are still weak and sinful, as Jesus makes very clear in many of his stories (the Prodigal Son [Luke 15:11–32], the woman "who was a sinner" [Luke 7:36–50], and the tax collector and the Pharisee [Luke 18:9–14], for example).

A mystical or unitive moment is not something that can be accessed by the left brain, but rather by the whole brain—right and left—and the heart and the body and the soul together. It is an intuitive grasp of the whole by the whole. That is what makes it so convicting and transformative.

God is another word for the heart of everything and for every-thing precisely in its connectedness. When we say we love God, we are saying we love everything. Immature religion becomes an excuse for not loving a whole bunch of things and reveals that we have not yet had an authentic God experience. All unloving reli-gion, including rigid religion and compulsive religiosity, are clear signs that we have not met God. Once we have had a unitive experience with God, Reality, or even ourselves, our life invari-ably shows two things: quiet confidence and joyous gratitude.

That's why mystics can love their enemies, the foreigner, and the outsider. They don't make the distinctions that low-level reli-gion does. Low-level religion is more tribal, a social construct to hold an individual group together. Some believe "I'm Catholic because I'm Irish" or "I'm Catholic because I'm Italian." This is just group identification and not even close to mystical expe-rience. In fact, this often becomes an avoidance of experience, as Jesus says to his own Jewish compatriots who tried to claim superiority because they were "sons of Abraham" (Luke 3:8). He even seems to say that the stones beneath his feet could be more fruitful than such futile reliance upon group or blood affiliation (Matthew 3:9).

Organized Religion and the Mystical Path

Organized religion is an example of incarnation. We have to start with the particular to go to the universal. We have to start with the concrete. In fact, we need a holding tank, a container to hold us in one spot long enough to learn what the real questions are and to struggle with them. That's what organized religion does for us. Some form of religion is necessary to carry on the Big Tradition, to give us the right words, to explain why mystical experience is even desirable or in any way possible. Otherwise, we have to start from zero and go in all sorts of ridiculous directions, as often happens with the unchurched today. Organized religion is an accountability system that holds our feet to the fire long enough for us to know what the issues really are, who God might be, and what our own limitations might also be.

So, in my vocabulary (and that's all it is), organized religion is very good and almost entirely necessary for what I call the first half of life.[1]

Now, the trouble is that organized religion usually tells us that mystical union with God is possible, but we should not really expect it. We're told that's only for special people. This ends up making mystical moments something very elitist, distant, and available to only a few now and then.

Organized religion often becomes problematic—not wrong, but problematic—when we move into the second half of life because it tends, in most instances, not to answer the questions that the soul is asking. Many people have found support in various forms of parachurch, like the Franciscans. But not everybody is called to be a priest, or a nun, or even a Third Order Franciscan. We need to find some way to learn, study, and pray alongside our Sunday worship community. Some are calling such parachurch groupings the "emerging church."[2] The Sunday service alone seldom leads people on deeper, or even real, journeys. We must be honest about this.

All that organized religion can do is to hold us inside the boxing ring long enough so we can begin to ask good questions and expect bigger answers. But it seldom teaches us how to really box with the mystery itself. Organized religion does not tend to finish the process. It doesn't teach us how to expect the mystery to show itself at any profound level. I don't mean to be unkind, but it tends to make us codependent upon its own ministry instead of leading us to know something for ourselves, which is really the whole point.

It's like we priests keep saying, "Keep coming back, keep coming back, and you'll eventually get it." But you don't because the whole thing is oriented toward something you attend or watch and not to something you can participate in all the time, even without the ministrations of priest, ministers, and formal sacraments. Again, I mean no disrespect. If God-experience depends on formal sacramental ministry from ordained clergy, then 99.9 percent of creation has had no chance to know or love God. That can't be true.

Moreover, if the clergy themselves have not gone on a further journey, they don't know how to send you there or guide you there because they have not yet gone there themselves (see Matthew 23:13). "*Nemo dat quod non habet*," we said in Latin: "You cannot give away what you do not have."

THE MYSTICAL PATH AND DAILY LIFE

Father Karl Rahner wrote of "the mysticism of daily life." We've got to stop making mysticism something that happens only to celibates, ascetics, and monastics.

That's precisely what Francis came to undo in order to bring religious life back to the streets, the laity, and the normal parish. People there have always been made to feel like third-class citizens of the Reign of God.

We do need to be given a new operating system. We cannot approach our daily work, our job, or our family with the dualistic mind: the judgmental, comparative, competitive mind, in which most of us are entirely trained—so much so that we think it is the only mind.[3]

Jesus refers to this as the judgmental mind. That's why he says, "Do not judge" (Matthew 7:1). Maybe we would simply say, "Do not label" things. It is just a way of trying to take control and often a game of superiority. The judgmental mind tries to know everything by merely comparing it to something else, which is to start with a negative first step. It is far removed from knowing things in themselves, by themselves, and for themselves. Such low-level attempts at knowing will never get us anywhere close to mystical experience. That's the simplest way to explain why the great spiritual teachers always convey some form of "Do not judge." The judgmental mind is too self-referential and closes down the open horizon right away.

The original word for this different mind, this alternative consciousness, was simply *prayer*. That word has been misused and trivialized to mean merely petitionary prayer, reading prayers, social prayer (liturgy), or reciting prayers. I'm afraid we Roman Catholics are well known for that: learning formulas and reciting them. Many of us teachers had to replace the word *prayer* with the word *contemplation* to communicate that we are talking about something different.

I'm not saying that formulaic prayer is wrong, but that is not what was taught by the Desert Fathers and Mothers in the first three or four hundred years of Christianity. That's not the original meaning of prayer. We see this from Jesus' many and long forays into the desert alone. Remember, the disciples had to coax him to teach them what we call the Our Father (Luke 11:1–4). Jesus is not known for temple prayer or social prayer, although he surely would not have opposed it unless it became too ritualistic, legalistic, or transactional, as we see when he cleanses the temple (Matthew 21:12–13). The Gospel does say that Jesus and the disciples "sang psalms together" (Mark 14:26; Matthew 26:30), the Hallel (Psalms 113–118) which opened and closed the Passover meal.

Prayer is looking out from a different set of eyes, which are not comparing, competing, judging, labeling, or analyzing, but receiving the moment in its present wholeness and incompleteness. That's what I mean by contemplation. It takes years of practice to switch from our normally dualistic thinking and allow nondual, receptive prayer to become our primary mode of consciousness.

For many, prayer still means reciting Our Fathers and Hail Marys, and I'm not trying to put down such prayers, especially when they are the spoken fruit of deeper prayer. But I know Catholics that have said Our Fathers and Hail Marys all their lives, priests who have said Mass all their lives, and still do not know how to pray. That is not a judgment on them, because no one taught them any differently. What I feel is more a deep sadness, because I know that without access to the deeper stream, their lives, their celibacy, and their ministry will be more about function than unction, to paraphrase Pope Francis' words to a clergy gathering.

The goal of prayer, as any good Christian would agree, is to give us access to God and to allow us to listen to God and to actually hear God, if that does not seem presumptuous. But mostly, prayer is to allow us to experience the Indwelling Presence ourselves. Finally, we are not praying, but prayer is happening through us (see Romans 8:26–27), and we just allow and enjoy it.

The only way we can do that is to work to maintain an open field—and yes, it is work to remain open to grace. What a total paradox. However, it does not mean that grace cannot break through anytime and anywhere. In fact, that is the most common pattern, but we want to enjoy the fruits of grace constantly, not just now and then.

If we lead off with the left brain, with the judging, calculating, dualistic mind, we will not access the Holy because the only thing that gets in is what we already think, what we already agree with, and what does not threaten us. God is, by definition, unfamiliar, always mysterious, beyond, and more. If we aren't ready for more and for mystery, how can we possibly be ready for God? Our intake valve will be very tight and guarded.

Contemplation is nondual thinking. It emerges when we don't split the field of the moment between what we already know and what we don't already know, as if one is totally wrong, heretical, evil, or sinful. Unfortunately, dualistic thinking is the common mode of thinking. The evidence for that is just about everywhere, especially in religion and politics, which is why we cannot meaningfully talk in those split fields.

Can We Trivialize Prayer?

If a whole lot of people are praying for the same thing and apparently at the same time, then there is a tendency to think that prayer is going to bend the arm of God. "More is always better" is the operative assumption here. At this point, I'm not really loving or serving God; I'm trying to get God to be on my side and give me what I want. It necessitates neither love nor surrender, but it is just a well-disguised desire to be in control. The wonderful news, of course, is that God is already on our side, so such thinking is futile and a waste of time. It is another way to try to manipulate mystery, as if we could.

There is something compassionate about asking God to heal your grandmother—of course, that's beautiful. But it is still *you* in the driver's seat, trying to get God in your car as a passenger, when God alone can be trusted with the driving. So, first we must listen for God's possible will, and not ours, and then—and only then—can we pray in the Spirit.

Jesus warns us about this verbal prayer when he says, "Why do you babble on like the pagans do? God already knows what you need" (Matthew 6:7). He also warns us against telling God what God already knows better than we do (6:8). I must say that many times the formal prayers of the faithful at a Roman Catholic Mass sound more like announcements than actual prayer, especially given the fact that they are done in the third person and not addressed directly to God, as if God is in the room, which would lead us to pray in the second person. (You have to go to Pentecostal churches to hear that!) In that same Gospel, Jesus even warns us against too much public prayer (6:5), since it has too many social payoffs. We must be honest and admit that we have not followed Jesus' basic advice on prayer. In fact, we often directly disobeyed it.

Jesus does tell us to ask God for what we want (Matthew 7:7–11). He does seem to affirm what we call petitionary or intercessory prayer. Why did Jesus say such a thing? It's not that we should talk God into what we want. It's not to announce it to God, since God knows and cares about suffering more than we do.

I believe intercessory prayer is important because we need to hear our own thoughts and words out loud. We need to jump on board with what we hope is the will of God and what may well be the will of God. It is an exercise in participation, in unitive caring together with God: what Paul calls divine and human cooperation (Romans 8:28). God does not need our prayers as much as we need to say them to even know the deepest will and desire of God—and our own.

Our prayers are simply seconding the motion. The first motion is always from God's Spirit working in the soul, making us care about human suffering and need. When we pray sincerely, God has already spoken to us, and we are just saying yes to what God wants even more than we do. That is why prayer leads us to fall in love with God, because we know we are not doing this good thing. It is being done unto us and through us.

It also seems that we don't know our own needs, feelings, and thoughts until we speak them. So, we all must keep praying "with groans unutterable" (Romans 8:23) until our prayers match the much deeper caring of God, and we discover that our own will and God's will are finally the same.

Is Happiness on the Path of Mysticism?

Here is an image that many others have offered. We don't catch a butterfly by chasing it. We sit still, and the butterfly alights on our shoulder. We don't find happiness by directly seeking happiness because that leaves us too self-centered. It is still all about us at that point, although we don't know it yet. Maybe you've had days where you think, "I'm going to be happy today," and then you realize you are trying too hard. It is too self-conscious, too intentional. Ego consciousness is still steering the ship.

Remember what I mentioned earlier about the old mammalian brain? Deep contentment is something we drop into, not anything that we consciously work toward too hard. Have you noticed how the happiness of achieving a goal rather quickly passes, and all we do is create another, supposedly higher goal?

There is an inherent restlessness—and defeat—in the conscious seeking of happiness. Happiness is much more in the realm of gift and surprise, like an alighting dove or a tongue of fire, which is surely why these metaphors are used for the Holy Spirit.

Happiness is too often selfishly defined, and thus it never works for long. Like children, we first define happiness in a largely sensory way, like a satisfying meal, a beautiful hotel room, or a wonderful sexual experience, which is all understandable. But those things, of themselves, do not make us happy. If we don't bring happiness into the hotel room, we're not going to be happy. We will just be pleased for a few minutes. But if we are already happy, we can be in a mediocre hotel room, or even in a not-so-nice hotel room, and we will still be able to say, "I'm happy and content today."

Sometimes simple things can give us even more and deeper happiness, precisely because we know that we are drawing upon a deeper well and stream—which can be accessed all the time, even without a five-star meal or fantastic sex.

Happiness is always a gift that comes from first seeking union or love. If love is our actual and constant goal, we can never really fail, and happiness comes much more easily and naturally. Please think about that, and you will know it is true.

The purifying goal of mysticism is divine union and nothing less. The goal of prayer is divine union—union with what is, with the moment, with ourselves, and with the Divine, which means with everything. Such things as healing, growth, and happiness are admittedly wonderful byproducts of prayer, but they must not be our primary concern. This pollutes the process. We don't want to make the goal of mysticism or prayer our personal happiness. That keeps *me* as the reference point: "I want to be happy." This important purification of motivation is quite central, and because historically we Christians have not insisted on it, we have a lot of church involvement being nothing more than very well-disguised self-interest (high-premium fire insurance) and not the love of God at all.

As a priest, I am aware that most of the official prayers in the Roman Catholic Sacramentary are praying, in some form, "that I might go to heaven." It's as if there is no higher concern or greater need in the world than for my personal eternal livelihood! I do not know how priests continue to recite such self-centered and individualistic prayers day after day. If the rule is true that *lex orandi, lex credendi* ("the law of prayer is the law of belief"),[4] then it is no wonder that the Christian people have such a poor record of concern for the suffering of the world and have themselves initiated so many of the wars and injustices on this earth. We did not teach them how to pray!

We must first seek union with God, and with everything, and then the butterfly will most assuredly alight gently and firmly on our shoulder. Then happiness comes along as a wonderful corollary and conclusion, as a gift, as a rich icing on the now well-baked cake of life itself.

CHAPTER FIVE

The Path to Nondual Thinking

*There is a kind of existence in which meditation and commu-
nication, epiphanies and busyness, death and life, God and
not—all these apparent antinomies are merged and made into
one awareness. I am a long way from realizing such perception
myself, but I have lifted the lens to my eyes.*

—Christian Wiman

How do we learn to move away from dualistic thinking? How do
we learn nondualistic thinking or contemplation?

That is a good question, because we do have to learn it. Dualistic
thinking is so taken for granted in the Western world that we
just call it thinking. Any systematic teaching of contemplation
has been lost to the Western churches for most of five centuries.
No wonder we keep splitting apart, fragmenting into over thirty
thousand groups that call themselves Christian. We have lost the

superior mind and heart, or at least our ability to access it. No wonder Jesus said, "Be careful how you listen" (Luke 8:18).

We are all educated into dualistic thinking. We think being able to make distinctions is what it means to be intelligent or rational. Most of our college professors love to make distinctions for us and teach us how to do the same. We have lost the older tradition which stated that there are some things previous to— and even more important than—the making of distinctions. In fact, the distinguishing of everything from other things is part of the problem! Distinctions are largely made in the mind, with words, and that surely has many positive and necessary aspects. But it also carries a bit of untruth with it, because we would do well to first see the similarities and deep identities of things before we distinguish this from that. I like to say that we must start with yes and never with no.

Even ancient religion saw that its job was to introduce people to an alternative way of thinking, which might have been called shamanism or divination. The practicing of that other way of thinking we would now call meditation, contemplation, or just prayer. I am convinced it is what the original word *prayer* meant. We must use a different processor. We do not fully process the moment by judging it, analyzing it, or differentiating it. We do not need to make it special or oppositional. We first must respect anything for being exactly what it is before we adjust it with our mind according to our likes and dislikes. Like a clean mirror, we must reflect it back without any added distortion (read "judgments").

I think people in earlier centuries, living in an agrarian society perhaps, before the printing press and the huge production of words, had much easier access to nondual thinking. Now, we have minds flashing like strobe lights. We no longer have easy access to the contemplative mind. It takes more work than ever to get a clean mirror, and it is for that very reason that the work is so important. Yet few today have been taught how.

Roman Catholicism and Eastern Orthodoxy have a long tradition of teaching contemplation. I have often been invited by Protestants to teach it, because they never had it in their history or tradition. It was lost by the time of the Reformation. We Catholics are in a worse state today: we think that because we know the word *contemplation*, we also know how to contemplate. Even Catholic contemplative religious orders stopped teaching it to their own members, which was quite a loss indeed. Many must have lived very frustrated lives, although some learned it by pure grace, by love, and by suffering.[1]

Catholics and Orthodox Christians must retrieve their own tradition of this alternative consciousness, but most traditionalists today are not traditional at all! They know so little about the Big Tradition beyond the last four or five hundred years—usually only the last hundred years, or even just their own lifetimes. That is what happens when we move into a defensive posture against others. We circle the wagons around externals and non-essentials, and the first thing to go is anything interior or subversive to our own ego.

First, we have to know that we do have this contemplative tradition. It is very clear in the Desert Fathers and Mothers, in Celtic Christianity, in the *Philokalia* of the Eastern Church, in Evagrius Ponticus (345–399), and in the monastic history of the ancient orders, which sometimes taught it directly or indirectly (as did Dionysius, John Cassian, the famous monastery of St. Victor in Paris, Bonaventure, and Francisco de Osuna). Most of our mystics exemplified the contemplative tradition more than they could verbalize their experience of it. Maybe this is part of why we lost it, and why good theological and spiritual teaching is important.

We know that nondual consciousness was taught on the systematic level until as late as the eleventh and twelfth centuries, usually among Benedictines or Cistercians. The early Franciscans are still the beneficiaries of this more ancient understanding. The Rhineland Dominicans beautifully exemplify it, and the Carmelites regathered much of it at Mount Carmel from their ancient history in Palestine. Its final flower, even supernova, of expression is, of course, in Teresa of Ávila (1515–1582) and John of the Cross (1542–1591), who had to re-teach contemplation at great cost to themselves.

But after the fights of the Reformation, after the over-rationalization of the seventeenth- and eighteenth-century Enlightenment, we became very defensive. We Roman Catholics wanted to prove that we were smart and could win arguments. In such a conversation, we by and large took on a more rational form of thinking and covered it with pious Christian words. Our own doctrines were henceforth presented in a dualistic, argumentative, and apologetic way. It was no longer nondual consciousness, but entirely dualistic thinking about Christian doctrines. Most priests were educated this way until the much-needed reforms of Vatican II in the 1960s.

At this point, after almost five centuries of not systematically teaching or even understanding contemplation, we had to find schools, teachers, and books and develop a practice to unlearn the old mind. Most of us thought that contemplatives were just introverted, quiet types who liked to pray. It left us extroverts and "doing" types out in the cold. Yet once we begin to learn the contemplative mind, we realize it is almost the natural way of seeing—and we have unlearned it! It is quite natural, as we see in children before the age of six or seven, when they start judging, analyzing, and distinguishing things from one another.

In my case, I first experienced contemplation before I learned how to name it well or to recognize it as such. I sometimes thought I was being naïve or a foolish Franciscan, not taking my intellect seriously enough. Yet so many smart people in the church felt unspiritual to me. I do not know how else to say it. Beginning with Thomas Merton's teaching, contemplation has flowered in many of us over the last thirty-five years. Learning from teacher after teacher, from many traditions, I began to name and understand my own experience. If something is *this* true, then we know for sure that many people will have discovered it, even if they use different vocabularies or have different assumptions about its goal.

I think many come to the contemplative mind as the fruit of great suffering or great love. They simply find themselves thinking nondually, non-oppositionally, and in a non-argumentative way. They enjoy the inner peace of God. They come to know that they can enjoy God, enjoy life, and enjoy themselves, and that they do not need to pick fights in their brains. It is such a pleasant place to live. Read Philippians 2:1–5, in which the nondual mind is on full display. It leads St. Paul to quote the wonderful hymn in verses 6–11, where he declares that we have "the same mind which is in Christ Jesus." I believe the contemplative mind is the mind of Christ.

The Gospel Is about an Alternative Mind and Thus Alternative Behavior

I often use the term "alternative orthodoxy," a phrase I gained from my Franciscan tradition, having to do with our emphasis upon lifestyle more than verbal correctness. Francis wanted us to *act* the Gospel, to live lives that were simple, loving, joyful, and nonviolent. I believe the reason we lost this alternative orthodoxy is because we first lost our alternative consciousness. We read everything in terms of a kind of dualistic conformity, choosing one side of most questions, which kept us in the world of words instead of our own experience. It usually did not emphasize actual practice, or *orthopraxy*. The contemplative mind does not hide behind words. It is in immediate contact with reality, with people, with events as they are and without ideological analysis.

Alternative consciousness is largely letting go of our mind's need to solve problems, to fix people, to fix ourselves, or to rearrange the moment because it is not to our liking.

When that mind goes, another mind is already there waiting, already quietly in place. That is what I mean by an *alternative* consciousness, an alternative set of glasses through which we can see the moment. But we cannot experience the one without letting go of the other—at least for a while.

For most people who have thought dualistically all their lives, it feels like dying, it feels like losing, and it feels like letting go of control, which is exactly why our Roman Catholic mystics consistently called it "darkness" or "knowing by darkness." This is surely why a lot of people do not go to higher or more mature stages of prayer. They want light and not darkness. They like to think, and thinking is largely commenting and arguing in our brain between conflicting or competing ideas. But note that I stated we must let go of our dualistic mind, at least for a while. We eventually have to return there to get most ordinary jobs done—but we will now do them in a less compulsive or driven way.

I think the genius of the Dalai Lama and Buddhism is that they do not get lost in metaphysics and argumentation about dogmas and doctrines; they just do not go there. As the Dalai Lama says, "My only religion is kindness." We could dismiss that as mere lightweight thinking, until we remember that Jesus said the same: "This is my commandment: You must love one another" (John 13:34). It is our religion too, or at least it should have been.

The Dalai Lama is not saying anything we do not already know, at least on some level. People said the same thing about Mother Teresa. She would offer simple little one-liners, and people would go away quoting her or saying she changed their lives. Contemplation leads us to have simple, clear eyes, common-sense faith, and loving energy that makes whatever we say quite compelling. Ironically, it also allows us to deal with often complex issues with the same simplicity and forthrightness as we now see in Pope Francis.

That is why we all need to encounter people who are able to operate as an example, a role model for us. The East has always recognized that transmission of spirituality takes place through living models, whom they called *gurus, sanyasis, pandits,* or *avatars.* It is what Catholic and Orthodox Christians mean by *saints.* We cannot just get the good news through concepts, ideas, and theories. We need to see and feel a living incarnation. "She is doing it. He exemplifies it. It is therefore possible for me too." It is almost more a taste, a smell, or a touch than an idea. Recent Christianity has relied far, far too much on ideas instead of living models. Sincere Christians can smell holiness, even when the words might seem unorthodox. They can also smell unholiness, even from people who do it all perfectly!

What I am stating here is that it can work the other way around too. Alternative behavior also helps create the alternative mind. We do not think ourselves into a new way of living, but we live ourselves into a new way of thinking. This is one of the core principles at our Living School for Action and Contemplation in Albuquerque, New Mexico.

It is very interesting that in the Eastern Church, most bishops and teachers, and many priests, were monks first. People such as Gregory of Nyssa, Gregory Nazianzen, Gregory Palamas, Basil, Athanasius, Cyril, and Evagrius Ponticus come to mind. In other words, those who first lived contemplation with some serious-ness had the authority to talk about it. This is an emphasis that we might well rediscover in our time. Most priests are ordained today by saying the right words, but without a single instance of having brought another person to faith, hope, or love. We have thus far been totally unsuccessful in getting a single seminary of any denomination to have a contemplative emphasis or curriculum.

Every time the Church divided—between East and West, and again as a result of the Reformation—we lost part of the whole message. That is how I see it. Further, in subsequent centuries, the neglected parts of the Gospel had to take shape in totally separate denominations which, thank God, preserved some gems, but usually missed some others. I wonder if any one denomination will ever be able to preserve all aspects of the great mind of Christ? Maybe human nature is only prepared to pay attention to a few select things.

Whenever we see a movement into solitude, hermitage, quiet, or any kind of aloneness, we know that we have nondual contemplative consciousness reemerging. You cannot spend days, weeks, and months alone unless your mind is different. The dualistic mind goes crazy and gets bored and angry with that much silence and solitude, while the nondual mind cannot get enough of it.

Whenever we see the reemergence of hermits, anchorites, and divisions in religious orders taking place over how to pray, we know that nondual consciousness has been rediscovered. This pattern is especially clear in the Benedictines, Carmelites, Augustinians, and Franciscans. It is at the core of every break and reform in these orders, although sometimes the interior poverty that contemplation demands gets confused with fights over external poverty in each of these groups—whether they were shod or discalced, or how much they fasted, etc. This is a common mistake.

In Spain, we have a lesser-known Franciscan friar and spiritual teacher, Francisco de Osuna (1497–1541), influencing Teresa of Ávila in this contemplative way. She called him her "greatest teacher." She recounted how, before she discovered him, mental prayer (which is what they called it then) was driving her crazy because she knew she could not control this compulsive, repetitive, obsessive thing that we call thinking. They still called it mental prayer when I was a novice in 1961, but it was largely about concentrating—which, of course, does not work. Most gave up on prayer very early—without realizing that they had. I am surprised that more people did not leave religious life.

Our father Francis showed all the evidence of being a supreme contemplative. Many who loved him in the first generation of Franciscans, like Brother Elias, did not know what to do with him. Francis was so simple and naïve to their dualistic way of thinking, yet there was an inner core of friars that accompanied him to the Carceri and hermitages for needed structural protection. These were probably Brothers Leo, Giles, Masseo, Rufino, and maybe even Juniper.

Then we have the intellectual masters, like Bonaventure and Scotus, who could maintain their simplicity while also giving the contemplative mind some intellectual rigor. There we have the best of both worlds, at least for educated people. Chapter seven of Bonaventure's *The Soul's Journey into God* (*Itinerarium Mentis in Deum*) is a succinct summary of what we now call Centering Prayer or the contemplative mind.

After the so-called Enlightenment of the seventeenth and eighteenth centuries, we had no room for contemplation because it appeared really naïve, as though we were just non-critical thinkers and pious lay brothers. Social prayer, specifically the Office and the Divine Liturgy, pretty much held the Roman Catholics and religious together in their respective groups. Unfortunately, it often became both a substitute and even an avoidance of an actual inner life. Daily Mass was our prayer, which became sentimentalized and dressed up, and often high theater, to offer us a false feeling of communion, intimacy, and mystery. These are the very gifts that are offered generously in contemplation, but in a way that goes deep and that lasts.

So has the pattern unfolded in our tradition. People only discovered contemplation by grace and accident. Thank God, there are usually quiet, hidden examples of such enlightenment in every community, including all those with which I have ever worked.

A Timeline of Mysticism

2500 BCE: First appearances of a sense of a loving, personal relationship with God in India and Egypt; "Original Participation" (Owen Barfield)

2000–1200 BCE: Abraham, Jacob, Elijah in Israel; Early Hinduism

600 BCE: Lao-Tzu

500 BCE: "The Axial Age" (Karl Jaspers); Buddhism is born; Socrates in Greece; Plato; the Upanishads in India

400 BCE: Taoism (*Tao Te Ching*) spreads in China

200 BCE: The Yoga Sutras of Patanjali in India; Jewish Apocalypticism, Book of Psalms, Song of Songs

30 BCE: Philo of Alexandria, a Jew in the Diaspora

First Century CE: Jesus of Nazareth, the first nondual teacher for the West; Paul's Letters, John's Gospel, "Present and Final

Participation" is promised and exemplified, which thrills Western civilization

Second Century: Clement of Alexandria (first to use the word *mysticus* or "hidden")

Third Century: Origen (Father of the Church), Plotinus (Roman philosopher)

Fourth Century: Basil, Gregory of Nyssa, and Gregory Nazianzen in Turkey; Evagrius Ponticus; Augustine; John Cassian; Macarius the Great; Desert Fathers and Mothers in Egypt, Syria, Cappadocia/Asia Minor, and Palestine; Trinitarian thinking is possible and highly valued (the "Principle of Three" allows and teaches nondual thinking)

Sixth Century: Benedict of Nursia (organizes the possibility of mysticism), Pseudo-Dionysius (apophatic way), Gregory the Great; Buddhism

Seventh Century: John Climacus, Maximus the Confessor: *Hesychasm* gives Orthodox Christianity a strong mystical basis; Theosis/divinization; Zen Buddhism in Japan and Tibetan Buddhism

Eighth Century: Rabia in Iraq; Shankara in India

Ninth Century: Little happening in Western Christianity, which appears to be dying along with the Roman Empire, except for Celtic monks outside the Empire, who begin to evangelize the continent

Tenth Century: Symeon the New Theologian in the East

Twelfth Century: Hugh and Richard of St. Victor, Aelred of Rievaulx, Bernard of Clairvaux, Hildegard of Bingen, William of St. Thierry (monastery-based)

Thirteenth Century: Explosion of mysticism: Francis and Clare of Assisi, Meister Eckhart, Beguines and Beghards, Bonaventure, Gertrude, Mechtilde, Hadewijch, Giles of Assisi, Angela of Foligno, Ramon Lull, many Franciscan hermits, German Dominicans Henri Suso and Johannes Tauler; Rumi and Ibn 'Arabi (Sufi master teachers)

Fourteenth Century: Jan van Ruysbroeck, Gregory Palamas, the anonymous author of *The Cloud of Unknowing*, Julian of Norwich, Catherine of Siena, Catherine of Genoa, Walter Hilton, Thomas à Kempis, Richard Rolle; Hafiz

Fifteenth Century: Nicholas of Cusa (coincidence of opposites), Francisco de Osuna, Nicholas of Flüe; Kabir (Hindu and Sufi holy man)

Sixteenth Century: The last mystical supernova: Ignatius of Loyola, Teresa of Ávila, John of the Cross, Francis de Sales, Jacob Boehme, Desiderius Erasmus (Most church reformations are born of extreme dualistic consciousness.)

Seventeenth Century: Crisis and decline: sweet piety or reason as a substitute for contemplation; the Enlightenment presented as the full triumph of dualistic thought; the "Desert of Non-Participation" begins (Owen Barfield); Brother Lawrence, George Fox, and Blaise Pascal, along with many women mystics who never attained prominence precisely because they were women and not taken seriously or allowed to be literate

Eighteenth Century: Jean Pierre de Caussade, John Wesley, William Blake, Seraphim of Sarov; Emmanuel Swedenborg; Hasidic Judaism and Baal Shem Tov

Nineteenth Century: Thérèse of Lisieux, Charles de Foucauld; Henry David Thoreau and William Wordsworth (the nature mystics)

Twentieth Century: rediscovery of "Participation": Friedrich von Hugel, Mahatma Gandhi, Evelyn Underhill, Thomas Kelly, Howard Thurman, D. T. Suzuki, Bede Griffiths, Rainer Maria Rilke, Elizabeth of the Trinity, Martin Luther King Jr., Alan Watts, Simone Weil, Thomas Merton; Thich Nhat Hanh, Rinzai Zen; Martin Buber, Etty Hillesum, Dag Hammarskjöld, Anthony de Mello, Ken Wilber, Gerald May, Ramana Maharshi, Pierre Teilhard de Chardin, Hugo Enomiya-Lassalle, Abraham Heschel, Rabindranath Tagore, Ruth Barrows, John Main, Eckhart Tolle, Bernadette Roberts, Paramahansa

Yogananda, various *rinpoches* and *gurus*, Henri Le Saux (Swami Abhishiktananda), Karl Rahner, Helen Keller, Mother Teresa (Saint Teresa of Calcutta), Dalai Lama (admittedly, this is an arguable and incomplete list)

What is emerging in the twentieth and twenty-first centuries is a major interface between East and West, the "two hemispheres of the Body of Christ": a rediscovery of nondual thinking, acting, reconciling, boundary crossing, and bridge building— based on the inner experience of God.

A Second Axial Age might just be emerging.[1] Yes, some is immature, some is syncretistic, some is ungrounded, some is not integrated, but the steps toward maturity are always and necessarily immature. The Holy Spirit is still evolving consciousness and teaching us how to pray.

NOTES

INTRODUCTION

1. *Nostra Aetate* (Declaration on the Relation of the Church
to Non-Christian Religions), 1, 2, https://www.vatican.
va/archive/hist_councils/ii_vatican_council/documents/
vat-ii_decl_19651028_nostra-aetate_en.html.

2. *Nostra Aetate*, 2.

3. Augustine of Hippo, *The Retractions*, trans. M. Inez Bogan,
Vol. 60, The Fathers of the Church (Baltimore: Catholic
University of America Press, 1968), 52.

4. *Optatam Totius* (Decree on Priestly Training), 15, https://
www.vatican.va/archive/hist_councils/ii_vatican_council/
documents/vat-ii_decree_19651028_optatam-totius_en.html.

5. Aldous Huxley, *The Perennial Philosophy* (New York: Harper
& Brothers, 1945), vii.

6. Julian of Norwich, *The Showings of Divine Love*, chapter 9.

7. Julian of Norwich, *The Showings of Divine Love*, chapter 65.

8. Julian of Norwich, *The Showings of Divine Love*, chapter 51.

CHAPTER ONE

1. Richard Rohr, *The Naked Now: Learning to See as the Mystics
See* (New York: Crossroad, 2009), chapter sixteen.

2. Cynthia Bourgeault and Richard Rohr, *The Shape of God:
Deepening the Mystery of Trinity* (Albuquerque, NM: Center for
Action and Contemplation, 2004), recording.

3. For more on Wilber's stages of growth, see Ken Wilber, *A Theory of Everything: An Integral Vision for Business, Politics, Science and Spirituality* (Boston: Shambhala, 2000).

CHAPTER TWO

1. Bourgeault and Rohr, *The Shape of God*.
2. Karl Rahner, *The Trinity* (New York: Crossroad, 1999), 10.
3. Rohr, *The Naked Now*, chapter two.

CHAPTER FOUR

1. Richard Rohr, *Falling Upward: A Spirituality for the Two Halves of Life* (San Francisco: Jossey-Bass, 2011), chapter three.
2. Richard Rohr, *What Is the Emerging Church?* (Albuquerque, NM: Center for Action and Contemplation, 2009), recording.
3. Rohr, *The Naked Now*, chapters four through six.
4. Historically adapted from Prosper of Aquitaine, *Patrologia Latina*, vol. 51, 209–210.

CHAPTER FIVE

1. Rohr, *The Naked Now*, chapter sixteen.

APPENDIX

1. Ewert H. Cousins was the first to suggest a Second Axial Age in his *Christ of the 21st Century* (New York: Continuum, 1992).